Surviving FINANCIAL ACCOUNTING

A HOW-TO GUIDE

KELLY F. GAMBLE
Ph.D., CPA, CGMA
Valdosta State University

Kendall Hunt
publishing company

Cover image © Shutterstock.com

Kendall Hunt
publishing company

www.kendallhunt.com
Send all inquiries to:
4050 Westmark Drive
Dubuque, IA 52004-1840

ISBN 978-1-5249-1651-0

Published in the United States of America

Dedicated to my mother

BEFORE WE BEGIN...

The materials contained in this book are not intended to be a replacement of, or substitute for, attending class, reading text assignments, practicing homework problems, or any other tasks or assignments given by your instructor. This book is designed to assist business students with developing the skills they will need to successfully complete their Principles of Financial Accounting courses. The author does not provide any guarantees with regard to educational outcomes or course grades.

Preface

AWAY WE GO...

Accounting has been called the "language of business." I have been teaching financial accounting principles to college students for over fifteen years. During that time, I have found that my students have had extremely varied backgrounds and levels of anxiety as they began their accounting studies. You may be taking the course for the first time, or you may be repeating the course after not achieving a desired grade on your first attempt. Or, perhaps you are a "nontraditional" student who has taken an accounting course several years ago and you are taking it again as a refresher course. You may even be a graduate student taking an accounting class as a prerequisite for your MBA program.

Whatever your background is, my goal in writing this book is to help you develop and practice the skills which are so important in achieving success in your accounting class. The practice problems contained in this book focus on solving accounting word problems, but the analytical skill you are working to develop in this course will be an asset to you in virtually any course of study or career path.

Developing analytical skills requires time and dedicated practice. No one can offer you a magic pill to make the process any faster or easier. The human brain is capable of amazing things, but, as with acquiring a physical skill (like tennis or dancing), regular training is necessary for skill mastery. This guide should be viewed as a tool in the process of training your brain to pick things apart in order to solve problems.

The topics included in this guide are the ones that tend to be confusing to accounting principles students. *You will need to rely on your course materials for full coverage of your course topics.* My intent is to provide you with alternative explanations and practice opportunities for some of the more complex topics.

Acknowledgments

I wish to thank several individuals and entities for their support and assistance with this project. First, thanks to all of my present and former financial accounting students for helping me to identify how a study guide like this one may help to fill in some missing pieces. I thank those who gave these pages a "test drive" and provided valuable feedback. I also thank the faculty and staff of the Langdale College of Business Administration at Valdosta State University for seeing the value in this type of publication. In addition, I must thank my PhD Project family and the KPMG Foundation for their many years of financial and academic support.

Table of Contents

INTRODUCTION – WHY DO I HAVE TO TAKE THIS CLASS? 1

SECTION ONE – WORKING THROUGH THE DETAILS 5

1. Understanding and Using the Accounting Equation 7
2. The Dreaded Debits and Credits 15
3. Those Annoying Adjusting Entries 21
4. What Are Financial Statements? 29
5. Closing the Books 33
6. Reconciling Bank Statements (This Can Save You Money!) 37
7. Demystifying Receivables 41
8. Inventory Issues 47
9. What Depreciation Is (and Is Not) 55
10. Liabilities (We Owe, We Owe, So Off We Go...) 59

SECTION TWO – A FEW MORE THINGS 63

11. Practice Solutions 65
12. Suggested Study Plan 79

Introduction

"Why Do I Have to Take this Class?"

This is a question I've been asked more times than I can remember. Most of the time, the student asking is a business major who has no plan to become an accountant. Believe me when I tell you that your professor knows that most of the students in an accounting principles course are nonaccounting majors. He or she is also aware that the majority of the students in the course would rather be almost anywhere than sitting through an accounting class. Unfortunately, your professor can't single-handedly modify your curriculum of required courses to exclude accounting. The fact is, principles of accounting is required of (dare I say) all business majors, and that fact is not going to change any time soon.

So, you're probably still wondering "why?" As I stated in the preface to this book, accounting is considered to be the language of business. For that reason, those who expect to become business professionals, regardless of the specific business function, must become "conversant" in that language. Suppose you moved to another country and you refused to learn the primary language. Would you expect to live a happy and successful life under those conditions? Probably not.

Accounting touches every aspect of business. Please take a look at the lists below. I've presented some examples of how accounting information is used by professionals in various business functions.

© Pressmaster/Shutterstock.com

Finance:

- Capital management
- Trend analysis
- Forecasting
- Debt versus equity financing

Information Systems:

- Budgeting
- Purchasing decisions
- Project management
- Staffing decisions

Management:

- Employment decisions
- "Make-or-buy" and "Buy-or-lease" decisions
- Mergers and acquisitions
- Outsourcing decisions

Marketing:

- Product-mix decisions
- Trade show and other promotional decisions
- Advertising budget decisions
- Product development and pricing

These lists are, by no means, exhaustive. The intent is to show how you might use the material you learn in your accounting classes after you graduate. Hopefully you can see that having a basic understanding of accounting is important to professionals in all areas of business.

Even if I have not yet convinced you, you are enrolled for the class so I'd suggest that you try to make the best of it. Telling yourself things like, "I hate this class" or "I'll never understand this stuff" is not productive. The reality is that you will have to take several classes that you don't believe you "need" over the course of your college career. For me, it was "Greek and Roman Mythology." To this day, that class has only helped me on a few Jeopardy!® questions. Please try to maintain a positive attitude whenever you find yourself in such a situation. I also strongly recommend the following:

- Read the textbook before going to lecture.
- Seek help as soon as you identify a problem.
- Ask questions in class.
- Form study groups.
- Practice as many problems as you can.
- Attend class regularly.
- Take good notes in class.

I've structured this book to help you build good study habits as you work through your accounting course. The main section of this guide focuses on the topics typically covered in principles of financial accounting courses. Each chapter is independent so that you can go directly to the area(s) in which you are interested. The third section contains many of the questions I've been asked most often by beginning accounting students along with a suggested study plan.

You will soon be introduced to Phyllis, the bookkeeper. Phyllis is a very sweet and friendly person, but she is not very good at her job. We will be called upon to correct Phyllis' errors and answer her questions as they arise.

I've also included several *"Need to Know"* boxes throughout the book. Understanding the concepts contained within these boxes is critical to your success in your accounting course. I've also included several examples to help you along the way.

As a final word of advice, I'd like to encourage you to spend as much time as you need outside of class studying this subject matter. *Accounting is not a subject that one can learn just by scanning the book, showing up in class, and writing down whatever your professor says.* Learning accounting takes time and practice. The grades students ultimately earn in these courses are generally a direct reflection of the amount of time and effort they put into learning the material.

So, let's get started!

© pzAxe/Shutterstock.com

Phyllis the bookkeeper

SECTION ONE

WORKING THROUGH THE DETAILS

Understanding and Using the Accounting Equation

1

What is Financial Accounting?

Financial accounting is a system which provides decision-useful financial information to interested parties to assist them in making resource allocation decisions. That may seem like a complicated definition, but it is really a simple concept.

For example, imagine that you have $1,000 and you want to invest in the common stock of either Walmart or Target. In order to make a fully informed decision, you would probably like to know how each company has performed over the last few years. Imagine if you had to look at every sales receipt from every store for the last year to determine how well the stores performed. The sheer volume of data would be overwhelming. This is where financial accounting becomes invaluable. It summarizes, in a concise way, all of the transactions into four financial statements (reports) that allow the readers to clearly see the results of operations, what the company owns, how much debt it has, and so forth.

Learning Key Terms

Among the first topics covered in a typical principles of accounting textbook is the analysis of transactions and the determination of their effects on the firm's financial position. Before we go any further, it is essential that we are comfortable with some definitions. Please spend some time learning and understanding the terms listed in **"Need to Know" (NTK) Box 1-1**.

Need to Know Box 1-1

ACCOUNT CLASSIFICATIONS

ASSETS

Items or objects that are:

1. owned by the corporation; and,
2. expected to provide future economic benefit

Examples: cash, buildings, machinery, furniture

(*Continued*)

(*Continued*)

LIABILITIES

Amounts the company owes to others. Liabilities represent the company's debt, and may be comprised of cash, goods, and/or services. Liabilities represent the creditors' claims to the company's assets.

Examples: accounts payable, salaries and wages payable

(STOCKHOLERS') EQUITY

Equity represents the owners' (stockholders') claims to the company's assets. Equity is often referred to as "residual ownership," because it represents the assets remaining after the creditors have been satisfied. Stockholders' equity has two components:

COMMON STOCK: represents contributed capital (i.e., amounts invested by owners); and,

RETAINED EARNINGS: represents earned capital (i.e., amounts earned by the corporation that are kept within the company and not distributed as dividends)

We also have an account called *DIVIDENDS*. Dividends are distributions of the firm's earnings to shareholders. Dividends are classified as "contra-equity" accounts* because they are directly subtracted from retained earnings. Dividends are NOT expenses (see next)

REVENUE

Amounts the company earns by performing its business activities.

Examples: rent revenue, sales revenue, service revenue

EXPENSE

Costs incurred by the company in order to generate revenue.

Examples: utilities expense, rent expense, salary and wage expense

****NOTE: the prefix "contra" means opposite!***

Learning and understanding these terms are absolutely critical to success in your accounting course. You will have to be able to look at an account name and identify its type (i.e., how it is classified using one of the five terms in NTK Box 1-1) in order to complete the course with a grade of C or higher. Please make sure you are comfortable with these definitions before you proceed to the next section.

The Accounting Equation

The "accounting equation" is stated as follows:

> ***Need to Know Box 1-2***
>
> The Accounting Equation:
>
> ASSETS = LIABILITIES + STOCKHOLDERS' EQUITY

The accounting equation is a simple representation of the company's financial position at a specific point in time. It indicates the total assets owned by the company and how much of the assets can be claimed by the creditors (liabilities) and by the company's owners (stockholders' equity).

We keep this equation in balance at all times by following certain rules when we enter information into the accounting system. If this equation is ever out-of-balance, the accounting system will not generate useful information to the financial statement reader.

Let's look at an example that may help to clarify what the accounting equation is actually telling us. Imagine that Susan is ready to purchase her first home. She's found the perfect house in the perfect neighborhood, and she's agreed on a price of $200,000. She provides a down payment of $25,000 and signs a mortgage note to finance the balance of $175,000. On the purchase date, her "personal" accounting equation with regard to this transaction would look something like this:

COST OF HOUSE	=	MORTGAGE	+	DOWN – PAYMENT
200,000	=	175,000	+	25,000
(asset)		(liability)		(Susan's equity)

Notice that the left and right sides of the equation are equal (in balance). Translating this into words, the equation is telling us that Susan owns a home which had a cost of $200,000. Of the total cost, the bank (mortgage lender) claims $175,000 and Susan can claim $25,000 as her own. If the house was sold on this date, the bank would receive the first $175,000 of the sales proceeds because *the creditors always have to be satisfied first*. Any amount received in excess of total liabilities (i.e., the "residual" amount) would belong to Susan.

Analyzing Transactions

Throughout a company's accounting year, it will experience several important events. Some of these events are included in the financial statements while others are not. Please review the terms in **NTK Box 1-3**.

Need to Know Box 1-3

EVENT

Something of significance that happens during a corporation's accounting period.

Example: signing an advertising contract

TRANSACTION

An EVENT (see above) that changes the corporation's financial position (i.e., affects the ACCOUNTING EQUATION (see NTK Box 1-2)).

Example: purchasing machinery for cash

ACCOUNT

A specific unit or item in the accounting system that is tracked in detail. All transactions that affect a particular account must be recorded so that the balance of the account can be updated.

Example: insurance expense, inventory, furniture and fixtures

The first step in the accounting cycle is analyzing transactions. This means that we must review all of the events that have occurred and determine whether or not they affected the firm's accounting equation (i.e., financial position) in any way. If so, then the event qualifies as a transaction that must be recorded in the accounting system.

Once transactions have been properly identified, we must go a step further by determining which accounts are affected and whether their balances are increased or decreased. One of the most frequent issues I encounter as an accounting professor is when students say, "I never know which account to use." As I stated earlier, mastering this process of analyzing transactions is *critical* in identifying the accounts that are affected. I have provided a list of commonly used accounts in **NTK Box 1-4.**

When analyzing events and transactions, I recommend the following thought process:

a. Read the EVENT description.
b. Translate the event into terms that allow you to clarify what "actually" happened.
c. Decide whether or not the EVENT qualifies as a TRANSACTION.
   - If the EVENT does not qualify as a TRANSACTION, it does not get recorded at all.
d. Determine the accounts that are affected by the transaction. *At least two accounts must be affected by each transaction* in order to keep the accounting equation in balance at all times.
e. Determine whether the balances in the affected accounts are increasing or decreasing (always from the corporation's perspective).
f. Show the effects of the transactions on the accounting equation.

Need to Know Box 1-4

SOME COMMONLY USED ACCOUNT NAMES
(not an all-inclusive list):

Assets	*Liabilities*	*S/H Equity*
Cash	Accounts Payable	Common Stock
Accounts Receivable	Notes Payable	Retained Earnings
Supplies	Salaries Payable	
Equipment	Utilities Payable	
Machinery	Interest Payable	

Revenues	*Expenses*
Sales Revenue	Rent Expense
Service Revenue	Interest Expense
Fee Revenue	Repairs and Maintenance Expense
Interest Revenue	Insurance Expense
Dividend Revenue	Supplies Expense

DEMONSTRATION

On January 1, Dr. John Robbins decides to open a new chiropractic practice, Spines, Inc. ("Spines"). He invests $50,000 into his new corporation in exchange for shares of common stock.

a. ***Read the problem description.*** (I will presume that you've read it already.)
b. ***What actually happened?*** John gave the corporation $50,000. In exchange, the corporation issued stock shares to him.
c. ***Is this event a transaction?*** (or, we can ask, does this event affect the accounting equation?) In this case, the corporation's assets and stockholders' equity are affected (see step b). Thus, this event qualifies as a transaction which must be recorded in the accounting system. Note: if the event is *not* a transaction, we would ignore it and move on to analyzing the next event.
d. ***Which accounts are affected?*** Based on step c, we can identify two accounts affected by this transaction: cash (asset) and common stock (stockholders' equity).
e. ***Are the account balances increasing or decreasing?*** The corporation is receiving cash from John, so its cash balance is increasing. The corporation is also issuing

new shares of stock to John which indicates that the balance in the common stock account is also increasing.

f. ***Show the effects on the accounting equation:*** this is the step that ensures our accounting equation stays in balance.

ASSETS	=	LIABILITIES	+	STOCKHOLDERS' EQUITY
+ $50,000 (cash)				+$50,000 (common stock)

Here, we can see that the total on the left side of the equal sign (+ $50,000) is the same as the total on the right side (+ $50,000). Hence, our equation is in balance, and we know which accounts are affected by the transaction.

PRACTICE 1-1

Instructions: use the 6-step method described earlier to analyze each of the following. If an event qualifies as a transaction, show its effect on the accounting equation (include the specific accounts affected).

- Jan 2: At his wife's urging, Dr. Robbins hires his sister-in-law, Phyllis, to be his bookkeeper. Phyllis will be paid $15 per hour. He also hired a physical therapist (at a salary of $40,000 per year), and an x-ray technician (with wages of $18 per hour).
- Jan 3: Spines paid $2,400 cash for a 12-month insurance policy.
- Jan 7: Spines purchased furniture for $10,000 "on account" (i.e., on credit; Spines has not yet paid for this purchase), and equipment for $25,000 cash.
- Jan 10: Spines purchased $5,000 of medical supplies on account.
- Jan 25: Spines paid for the furniture purchased on Jan 7.
- Jan 30: The total value of services provided to patients in January was $38,000. Of this amount, $30,000 was received in cash from Dr. Robbins' patients and the remaining amount was billed to patients at the end of the month.
- Jan 30: Spines paid his employees a total of $8.000 for the month of January (ignore taxes).
- Jan 30: Spines paid Dr. Robbins a dividend of $2,000.

Keep In Mind:

- When companies pay for something in advance (e.g., the insurance and supplies described earlier), they record the payment as a "prepaid" expense. The prepaid expense account (e.g., prepaid insurance or supplies) is classified as an asset and will be reclassified to an expense account as the item is "used up." This topic is covered in more detail in chapter 3.
- Purchases made "on account" indicate that the item has not yet been paid for.

- Transactions do not always affect one account on the left side and one account on the right side. For example, if the firm purchases an asset for cash, it is simply exchanging one asset for another. In this situation, the net change in total assets is zero, and the equation stays in balance.
- Some transactions affect three or more accounts.

A Few Words of Advice

As a final reminder regarding transaction analysis, it is *absolutely imperative* that you master this skill before moving forward in the course. You will need to be able to identify accounts and determine how they are affected by various transactions in order to earn a passing grade. *Repeated practice is the key!!* Use the practice questions contained in this book along with the materials provided with your textbook to help build your skill level. Please do not move forward until you feel comfortable analyzing transactions.

The Dreaded Debits and Credits

2

Now that you've mastered the process of analyzing transactions, the next step is to enter the transactions into the accounting system so that the account balances can be updated. We do this by applysing certain rules and structuring the transactions in a particular format.

I've found that many accounting principles students get very uncomfortable when our class discussions turn to the topics of debits and credits. In truth, the concepts of "debit" and "credit" are not difficult at all.

> ***Need to Know Box 2-1***
>
> "DEBIT" means left-side entry "CREDIT" means right-side entry

Your textbook probably uses "T-accounts" as a tool for tracking the activity in each account. They may look something like this:

ACCOUNT NAME	
Debit Side	Credit Side

With this figure in mind, "debiting" an account means that we enter a dollar amount on the left side and "crediting" an account means that we enter an amount on the right side. Right now, we have no way of knowing whether the account balance is increasing or decreasing. That depends on which type of account we are working on. Thus, your next task is to memorize the "normal balances" for the various account types (coming up soon).

To determine the balance in any particular account, simply add all of the debits and then add all of the credits. Find the difference between the two sides (i.e., the balance) and then present that figure on the side which is larger. Thus, if debits exceed credits, the account has a debit balance (the reverse is also true).

A Few More Definitions

I've listed a few more definitions next. Some of these may not match your previous experiences, but you will have to adapt to using these "accounting vocabulary words" in order to do well in the course.

- *Journal* (also called "general journal")—the entry-point for all transactions into the accounting system
- *Ledger* (also called "general ledger")—collection of all of the accounts in the system with all of the detailed information that affects the accounts' balances
- *Posting*—the process of transferring transactions from the journal to the ledger
- *Chart of accounts*—a list of all of the accounts in the system; does not include any transaction information or account balances
- *Trial balance*—a list of all of the accounts in the system along with their balances (shown in the debit column or credit column as appropriate)

Normal Balances

The term "normal balance" refers to the side of the account (i.e., the debit or credit side) that causes the balance of that account to increase. You can also think of the normal balance as the positive side of an account. I have provided a simple pneumonic device which you can use to help you remember the normal balances.

Need to Know Box 2-2

NORMAL BALANCE—the side of an account (either debit or credit) that causes its balance to increase.

"DEAD C[u]RLS"—a tip for memorizing normal balances

Debits increase	Credits increase
Expenses	Revenues
Assets	Liabilities
Dividends paid	Stockholders' Equity

You can think of the DEAD CRLS pneumonic as your debit and credit rules. Simply stated, it is telling you that the normal balance (positive side) of expense, asset, and dividend accounts is the debit (left) side. So, if we want to increase the balance in an asset account (like cash), we would use a debit. And, since we know that debits increase the balances in these accounts, we also know that these types of accounts are decreased with credits.

The opposite is true for revenue, liability, and stockholders' equity accounts. These types of accounts are increased with credits (right-side entries). Also, these types of accounts are decreased with debits.

It is imperative that you learn these rules very well and as soon as you can. Everything we do in the course from this point forward will draw upon your understanding of these normal balances and using them to prepare journal entries (coming up soon).

Journalizing and Posting

The general journal is where the transactions enter the accounting system. The process of preparing "journal entries" is called "journalizing." Journal entries have a very specific format. I will summarize our rules for preparing journal entries in "good form:"

- Each entry should have a date (far left) column
- In the second section, we see the accounts that are affected by the transaction we have analyzed.
- Rules for the preparation of journal entries:
  - All debited accounts are listed first along the left margin.
  - All credited accounts are listed after the debited accounts and are indented from the left margin (indicating that they are right-side entries).
  - Dollar amounts being debited are shown in the debit column; those being credited are shown in the credit column.
  - *Every journal entry must include at least two accounts. An entry may contain more than two accounts, but it can't contain only one.*
  - *For each journal entry, total debits MUST EQUAL total credits.*
  - A parenthetical explanation of the purpose of the entry may be included at the end of the entry.

Need to Know Box 2-3

JOURNAL ENTRY FORMAT

Date	Debited Account No. 1	$$	
	Debited Account No. 2	$$	
	(etc.)	$$	
	Credited Account No. 1		$$
	Credited Account No. 2		$$
	(etc.)		$$
	(Explanation/purpose of the journal entry)		

When we have journal entries that are comprised of only one debited account and one credited account, we call them "simple" entries. When an entry affects more than two accounts, we call it a "compound" entry. And remember, in ALL cases, the total of debits and credits must be equal for each journal entry.

The next step in the accounting cycle is to transfer the journal entries to the individual accounts in the general ledger so that their balances can be updated. This is called "posting."

Need to Know Box 2-4

Jan. 1: Dr. John Robbins decides to open a new chiropractic practice, Spines, Inc. ("Spines"). He invests $50,000 into his new corporation in exchange for shares of common stock.

Journalizing:

Jan 1	Cash	50,000	
	Common Stock		50,000
	(Record issue/sale of common stock)		

<u>Posting</u>:

CASH		COMMON STOCK	
50,000			50,000

As a result of Dr. Robbins investing $50,000 cash into Spines and receiving shares of stock in exchange, the practice has a $50,000 balance in its cash account and a $50,000 balance in common stock account. This process is repeated for each transaction that occurs during the accounting period.

PRACTICE 2-1

Instructions: journalize and post the transactions listed in PRACTICE 1-1. Omit explanations.

Unadjusted Trial Balance

The next step is to summarize the information contained in the general ledger in the form of a trial balance. Please refer to the example next.

Need to Know Box 2-5

TRIAL BALANCE EXAMPLE

ABC, Inc,
Unadjusted Trial Balance
as of January 31

Cash	40,000	
Accounts Receivable	2,000	
Prepaid Insurance	3,000	
Furniture	12,000	
Equipment	20,000	
Accounts Payable		6,000
Common Stock		25,000
Dividends	1,000	
Service Revenue		50,000
Rent Expense	1,000	
Salary and Wage Expense	2,000	
	81,000	81,000

This is the first of three trial balances that are prepared during the accounting period. Not surprisingly, this one is called "unadjusted" because it hasn't been adjusted yet (next chapter). You will find that each of the accounts is listed in the trial balance along with the account balances after all of the transactions have been posted. Please take note of a few items about the unadjusted trial balance:

1. The ordering of the accounts:
    1. Assets
    2. Liabilities
    3. Stockholders' equity
    4. Revenue
    5. Expenses
2. The total of the debit column equals the total of the credit column (if the columns do not agree, then an error has been made.

While the trial balance is helpful in proving that the accounting system is in balance, it is limited in helping us to determine if other types of errors have been made.

For example, the trial balance (presuming it is in balance) will not help to identify whether the following have occurred:

- A transaction was posted twice
- A transaction was omitted
- An incorrect account or amount was used when recording a transaction

PRACTICE 2-2

Instructions: Prepare the unadjusted trial balance for Spines, Inc. as of January 31.

Those Annoying Adjusting Entries

3

We have arrived at the point in the accounting cycle called "adjusting the accounts." Before getting into the details, let's discuss why we need to make adjustments in the first place. The simple answer is that we often encounter timing differences because we are following "accrual basis" accounting as opposed to "cash basis" accounting.

Accrual versus Cash-Basis Accounting

The concept that comes into play here is the Time Period Assumption (also called the Periodicity Assumption). In essence, accountants are assuming that time can be separated into individual accounting periods (one month, one quarter, one year, etc.).

The primary difference between accrual basis and cash basis accounting is when revenues and expenses are recognized. In accounting, the term "recognize" means that we record a revenue or expense and include it on the income statement (next chapter). This also means that the recognized item is a component of the net income calculation.

With cash basis accounting, *revenues are recognized when cash is received and expenses are recognized when cash is paid*. Although this is simple and straight-forward, it is not the method required for reporting under Generally Accepted Accounting Principles (GAAP). Here are a couple of reasons:

- Reporting under the cash basis doesn't give a full picture of what actually happened with the company during the accounting period; and,
- In accounting, whenever we have a choice between two methods (say, an easy one and a harder one), GAAP always requires the harder one (I'm only half-kidding).

We often encounter situations in which revenues are earned in one accounting period while the cash is received in another. Similarly, we often incur expenses in one accounting period while the cash is paid in another. Thus, we encounter the timing differences that I mentioned earlier. The adjusting process is necessary in order to ensure that all revenues and expenses are recognized in the appropriate accounting periods.

With accrual basis accounting, we must follow the revenue recognition principle and the expense recognition principle. When we follow these two rules, we are following what is called the matching principle. GAAP requires that we follow accrual basis accounting because it is more informative for the financial statement reader.

Need to Know Box 3-1

REVENUE RECOGNITION PRINCIPLE

Revenues are recognized in the period in which they are earned. Revenues are not considered earned until the company has completed its performance obligation(s).

EXPENSE RECOGNITION PRINCIPLE

Expenses are recognized in the same period as the revenues they helped to generate. We sometimes say that the "expenses follow the revenues." We also refer to this expense recognition principle as the matching principle. This is so because we are attempting to "match" the expenses with their related revenues.

ACCRUAL BASIS OF ACCOUNTING

Revenues are recognized in the period in which they are earned and expenses are recognized when incurred. In other words, revenues are "matched" with their related expenses.

Demonstration

ABC, Inc. reports the following activity for the month of January:

- Total sales for the month were $10,000. Of this amount, $6,000 was collected in cash, and the remaining $4,000 has not yet been received from customers.
- Total cash expenditures for the month were $2,500. ABC has also received bills totaling $1,500 that have not been paid as of month-end.

What is ABC's net income under both the cash and accrual bases of accounting?

	Cash Basis	Accrual Basis
Revenues	$6,000	$10,000
(Expenses)	(2,500)	(4,000)
Net Income	$3,500	$6,000

The cash basis net income figure is reporting how much cash was received from customers and how much cash was paid for expenses during the month. The accrual basis net income figure reports how much revenue was earned during the month (even though the full amount has not yet been received in cash). It also reports the amount of expenses incurred in the process of earning the revenues for the month (even though the full amount has not yet been paid in cash). Which of these net income figures do you consider to be more informative or meaningful?

Why Are Adjustments Necessary?

As I mentioned earlier, we are often faced with timing differences in accounting. A firm might earn revenue in one accounting period and receive cash in the next accounting period. Or, in the case of expenses, the firm may incur (i.e., use, consume, or get the benefit from something) in one accounting period, but pay for it in the next. Because we are following accrual basis accounting rules, we must make sure that all revenues and expenses are recognized in the proper accounting periods, regardless of when cash is received or paid.

For this reason, firms are required to "adjust" their account balances before they can issue financial statements. If a firm fails to make the appropriate adjustments, the financial statements they generate will likely be incorrect. Thus, the adjustment process is very important for providing useful and accurate information to both the internal and external users of the firm's financial statements.

Types of Adjustments

Following GAAP requires the preparation and posting of two types of adjustments: accruals and deferrals:

- *Accrual* adjustments are made when the firm has either earned revenue or incurred an expense before any cash has been exchanged.

Need to Know Box 3-2

ADJUSTING ENTRIES (A SUMMARY)

Prepaid (Deferred) Expense:		
Expense Account	$	
Asset Account		$
Unearned (Deferred) Revenue:		
Liability Account	$	
Revenue Account		$
Accrued Expense:		
Expense Account	$	
Liability Account		$
Accrued Revenue:		
Asset Account	$	
Revenue Account		$

- *Deferral* adjustments are made when a cash exchange has taken place before the firm has either earned revenue or incurred an expense.

Because accrual and deferral adjustments apply to both revenues and expenses, we have a total of four types of adjusting entries that might be needed.

Prepaid (Deferred) Expenses

In this situation, the firm has paid for something in advance and then uses it a little bit at a time. When a firm pays for something in advance, the amount is debited to an appropriately named asset account (prepaid rent, supplies, etc.). These prepayments are classified as assets because: (1) they are owned by the firm and (2) they provide future economic benefit. Recall these criteria from our definition of assets in Chapter 1.

As an example, recall that Spines paid $2,400 on January 3 for a full year of insurance coverage. As the payment is made, the firm would record the following journal entry:

January 3	Prepaid Insurance	2,400	
	Cash		2,400

Hopefully, you can agree that the full $2,400 payment will not be completely "used-up" by the end of January. Actually, the company will benefit from this payment for a full twelve months. Therefore, if the company prepares monthly financial statements, the amount of insurance coverage "used" during each month must be recognized as an expense on the income statement.

In this example, the insurance is used (or "expires") at a rate of $200 per month ($2,400/twelve months). Therefore, each month Spines must make the following adjusting entry:

January 31	Insurance Expense	200	
	Prepaid Insurance		200

The effect of this adjusting entry is to increase the amount of insurance expense recognized on the income statement (debit to insurance expense) while simultaneously reducing the balance in the prepaid expense asset (using a credit). After this adjusting entry has been posted on January 31, the balance in the insurance expense account is $200 (debit) and the balance in the prepaid insurance account is $2,200 (debit).

NOTE: Preparing adjusting entries requires strong understanding of the material covered in Chapters 1 and 2. If you haven't yet mastered the process and rules of preparing journal entries, please stop here and go back to Chapters 1 and 2 for review. Once you are comfortable with that material, please continue with Chapter 3.

A special type of prepaid expense adjustment is called *depreciation* (details are covered in Chapter 9). Unlike the definitions used in finance and economics courses, the accounting definition of depreciation is "a cost allocation process." Depreciation comes into play when a firm purchases an asset that it will use for more than one year. In these cases, we use a systematic method to allocate the cost of the asset to the accounting periods for which the asset helps to generate revenue. The adjusting entry to record depreciation looks like this:

Date	Account	Debit	Credit
Date	Depreciation Expense	$	
	Accumulated Depreciation		$

The accumulated depreciation account is a "contra-asset" account. It is listed with the assets, but has the opposite sign. The balance in the accumulated depreciation account is subtracted from the cost of its related asset to determine the asset's "book value" (i.e., the asset's undepreciated cost).

As you proceed through the adjustment process, it is quite likely that you will need to add accounts to your unadjusted trial balance. This is perfectly acceptable. Again, our intent is to make sure all revenues and expenses have been recognized properly. So, if some of the revenue and expense accounts were not on the unadjusted trial balance, we are correcting the balances by adding them during the adjustment process.

Unearned (Deferred) Revenues

Unearned revenues arise when a customer pays the company in advance of any work being done that would allow it to record revenue. An example would be a house painter who receives a $500 deposit from a customer on June 15, prior to beginning the painting job. In this example, the painter would record the following journal entry:

Date	Account	Debit	Credit
June 15	Cash	500	
	Unearned Service Revenue		500

By posting this journal entry, the painter records that he has received $500 cash, but since he has not yet done any work (i.e., he has not fulfilled his performance obligation), he can't classify the $500 as revenue. Therefore, he must record an "unearned revenue" account with a credit. This account is classified as a liability because the painter owes the customer one of two things: (1) painting service or (2) a refund if no service is performed.

Assume that by June 30, the painter has provided painting services worth $500 to this customer. The adjusting entry at month-end would look like this:

June 30	Unearned Service Revenue	500	
	Service Revenue		500

This adjusting entry reduces the balance in the Unearned Service Revenue account to zero (i.e., the full deposit has now been earned), and records the amount of revenue earned by performing painting services for this customer in June.

Accrued Revenues

Continuing with our painting example, imagine that the painter completes the job on July 8 and the total price of his painting service provided in July is $1,500. This means that he has earned $2,000 from this job: $500 in June and $1,500 in July. However, since the painter bills his customers at month-end, he does not expect to receive payment from this customer until August. As he generates a bill (i.e., accrues revenue) for the customer on July 31, he will record the following adjusting entry:

July 31	Accounts Receivable	1,500	
	Service Revenue		1,500

This adjusting entry serves several purposes.

1. The debit to Accounts Receivable records the amount the customer owes the painter. Note that this account is classified as an asset.
2. The credit to Service Revenue recognizes the fact that the painter has earned $1,500 for the services he provided during the month of July, even though he hasn't yet received full payment.

Presuming the customer pays the full balance on August 12, the painter will post the following journal entry:

August 12	Cash	1,500	
	Accounts Receivable		1,500

Please note that the painter is NOT recording revenue when the cash is received in August. The revenue was recorded in July when it was earned. When the cash is received in the next accounting period, the painter simply credits the customer's account receivable that brings the balance down to zero.

PRACTICE 3-1

Suppose the painter recorded the following journal entry when the customer paid the balance in August:

August 12	Cash	1,500	
	Service Revenue		1,500

What effect does this error have on the firm's financial position?

I encourage you to prepare T-accounts for these examples and make sure you understand how and why the balances in these accounts change the way they do.

Accrued Expenses

The last type of adjusting entry we will cover is accrued expenses. These occur when the firm has used (or gotten the benefit of) something that it has not yet paid for. As an example, assume that the painter receives a $350 utility bill on June 28 for the services it received during the month of June. The firm's next scheduled check-run is July 6. Thus, the painter will be paying for his June utilities in July. In this situation, the painter will have to accrue utility expense for June so that the expense is included on the June income statement, even though it won't be paid until July. The June 30 adjusting entry would look like this:

June 30	Utility Expense	350	
	Accounts Payable		350

The effects of this entry are to recognize the January utility expense in January and to record a liability (accounts payable) to let financial statement users know that the firm owes the utility company $350. When the bill is paid on February 6, Spines will make the following journal entry:

July 6	Accounts Payable	350	
	Cash		350

This journal entry reduces the balance in the liability account to zero and reduces the cash balance by the amount paid to the utility company. Note that Spines is not recording any additional expense on February 6 when the bill is paid. The utility expense was recorded in January when it was used.

PRACTICE 3-2

What if the painter recorded the following journal entry when he paid the utility bill in July?

July 6	Utility Expense	350	
	Cash		350

What effect does her error have on the firm's financial position?

Adjusted Trial Balance

Once all of the adjusting entries have been prepared and posted, the firm generates a second trial balance. This one, not surprisingly, is called the adjusted trial balance (can you guess why?). The format of the adjusted trial balance is the same as what we discussed when preparing the unadjusted trial balance. The adjusted trial balance may contain more accounts because some accounts could have been added during the adjustment process. The limitations we discussed also apply to the adjusted trial balance.

PRACTICE 3-3

Use the following information to prepare the necessary adjusting entries for Spines, Inc. on January 31. Post the entries and prepare an adjusted trial balance.

- Depreciation on the furniture is $600 per year.
- Depreciation on the equipment is $1,000 per year.
- A count of the supplies on January 31 indicates that $3,500 of supplies is still on hand.
- Spines received the following bills on January 30. They will be paid on February 7: telephone $80; utilities $250.

What Are Financial Statements? 4

Financial statements are the reports generated by the firm's accounting system. They summarize the operations and financial position of the firm for a specified date or accounting period. We usually focus on three financial statements in the accounting principles course:

Need to Know Box 4-1

FINANCIAL STATEMENT FORMATS

CORPORATION NAME
INCOME STATEMENT
FOR THE PERIOD ENDED DATE

Service Revenue	xx
Expenses	<xx>
Net Income	xx

CORPORATION NAME
STATEMENT OF RETAINED EARNINGS
FOR THE PERIOD ENDED DATE

Beginning Balance	
+/− Net Income <Loss>	xx
Dividends	<xx>
Ending Balance	xx

(*Continued*)

(*Continued*)

CORPORATION NAME

BALANCE SHEET

AS OF DATE

Assets	
List of assets	xx
Liabilities and Stockholders' Equity	
List of liabilities	xx
Common Stock	xx
Retained Earnings	xx
Total Liabilities and Stockholders' Equity	xx

1. The *Income Statement* is prepared first. This statements shows the results of the firm's operations during the accounting period. On the income statement, we find revenue accounts and expense accounts. Total revenues minus total expenses result in net income (positive result) or net loss (negative result). Please also note the *heading* of the statement. First, we see the name of the corporation; next, we see the name of the statement; and last, we see the time period being reported.
2. Next, we prepare the *Statement of Retained Earnings.* The heading for this statement is similar to the one we saw for the Income Statement, we just need to change the name of the statement. We start with the beginning balance of retained earnings (in the example, the beginning balance is zero because we are looking at a brand new corporation). We next add the net income (or subtract the net loss) for the period as calculated on the income statement. Finally, we subtract the dividends for the period. The result is the ending balance of retained earnings.
3. Finally, we prepare the *Balance Sheet.* The account types on the balance sheet are the same as what we see in the accounting equation (assets, liabilities, and stockholders' equity). Note in the heading that the balance sheet shows the firm's *financial position for a specific date,* not for an accounting period as we saw with the two statements discussed earlier. The balance sheet is like a photograph of the firm's resources (assets) and claims to those resources (liabilities and equity) on a particular day. Notice that the balance sheet is in balance. We forced this to happen by making sure our accounting equation remained in balance as we analyzed each transaction.

Classified Balance Sheet

As discussed earlier, the balance sheet contains asset, liability, and equity accounts. A "classified" balance sheet simply lists these accounts by subcategory. Here is a brief summary:

- Current assets—assets expected to be used, consumed, or converted to cash within one year (e.g., cash, accounts receivable, inventory)
- Long-term investments—assets expected to be used (or held) for longer than one year (e.g., stocks of other corporations, real estate not being used in operations)
- Property, plant and equipment—assets used in generating revenue and expected to be used for more than one year (e.g., machinery, furniture and fixtures, vehicles)
- Intangible assets—assets used to generate revenue but lacking in physical substance (e.g., patents, trademarks)
- Current liabilities—liabilities to be satisfied within one year (e.g., accounts payable, salaries payable)
- Long-term liabilities—liabilities to be satisfied in more than one year (e.g., mortgage payable, bonds payable)
- Stockholders' equity—described in an earlier chapter. The two parts of equity for a corporation are common stock and retained earnings.

PRACTICE 4-1

Prepare the financial statement for Spines for the month of January.

---

5 Closing the Books

Closing the books is the final step in the accounting cycle. When we say that an account is "closed," we mean that the balance of the account is set to zero. In order for an account to have a zero balance, its total debits must equal its total credits. Our objective is to transfer the revenue, expense, and dividend balances to the retained earnings account. Back in Chapter 1, we discussed the five different types of accounts (assets, liabilities, etc.). Now, we are going to further classify these account types into two groups:

- Temporary (or nominal) accounts—balances are closed at the end of the accounting period
- Permanent (or real) accounts—balances are rolled forward to the next accounting period.

The temporary accounts are revenues, expenses, and dividends. This should make sense since we've already seen that the balances in these accounts would be transferred to retained earnings at the end of the accounting period. Revenues and expenses are income statement accounts. The dividend account is a contra-equity account (i.e., an equity account with a debit balance). The permanent accounts are assets, liabilities, and equity accounts (the balance sheet accounts).

This should help you to remember which accounts get closed: balance sheet accounts keep their balances and roll them forward; income statement accounts are closed each period. Again, to make this more meaningful, think of your own bank account (an asset called "cash"). Let's say that you have $500 in your account on December 31, 2015. What happens to that balance on January 1, 2016? Does it go away or does it become your beginning cash balance for the year 2016? You can also think about your student loans or car notes (liabilities). Do the balances in those accounts on December 31, 2015 just disappear on January 1, 2016? Though we wish they would, those balances also roll into the next year. Sorry!

The closing process itself is relatively simple. The process uses an account called "Income Summary," which is a temporary account itself. Its purpose is just to "summarize" our revenues and expenses to determine the net income or net loss for the period. Here are the four steps:

1. Close all revenue accounts to Income Summary
2. Close all expense accounts to Income Summary
3. Close Income Summary to Retained Earnings
4. Close Dividends to Retained Earnings

Need to Know Box 5-1

CLOSING PROCESS

1.	Revenue Accounts	$$		
	Income Summary		$$	
2.	Income Summary	$$		
	Expense Accounts		$$	
3a.	Income Summary	$$		(Net income)
	Retained Earnings		$$	
OR				
3b.	Retained Earnings	$$		(Net loss)
	Income Summary		$$	
4.	Retained Earnings	$$		
	Dividends		$$	

To complete this process, you'll need to remember your DEAD CRLS (normal balance) rules. Revenue accounts have credit balances normally. Therefore, to close a revenue account, you'll need to debit the account for an amount equal to its credit balance. Each revenue account requires its own debit so that the balance of each revenue account is zero when we post the closing entry to the general ledger.

Similarly, since expenses have debit balances normally, each expense account is credited and the sum of the expenses is debited to Income Summary.

After step 2 is complete, Income Summary contains the totals of all revenues and expenses. We already know that the difference between revenue and expenses is net income or net loss. So, we now need to transfer this amount to retained earnings where it will remain until it is distributed as a dividend. If the firm has net income for the period (revenues exceed dividends), Income Summary will have a credit balance. Thus, to close Income Summary, it is debited for an amount equal to net income and then retained earnings is credited (resulting in an increase to retained earnings). If a firm experiences a net loss, the third closing entry would be reversed (i.e., debit to retained earnings, and credit to Income Summary—resulting in a decrease in retained earnings).

The final step is to close the dividends account. We learned earlier that dividends are distributions of the firm's earnings to the shareholders. Thus, dividends directly reduce retained earnings. We see this happen in the fourth closing entry. Retained earnings is debited while the dividend account is credited. Please take some time to make sure you understand this closing process.

Post-Closing Trial Balance

The very last thing we need to do is prepare a third trial balance. This one is called "post-closing" because we prepare it after the closing entries have been posted. This trial balance should contain only the permanent accounts (assets, liabilities, and equity). The balance in retained earnings should reflect the closing entries discussed earlier. If you see any revenue, expense, or dividend accounts on a post-closing trial balance, then a mistake was made somewhere!

PRACTICE 5-1:

Assume that January 31 is the year-end for Spines. Prepare the closing entries and the post-closing trial balance.

Reconciling Bank Statements (This Can Save You Money!) 6

One of the most important tasks for any company is to maintain control of its assets, especially cash. Firms use banks to help keep cash records and to keep its funds secure. While using a bank to process financial transactions provides several benefits (as opposed to keeping large quantities of cash on hand), errors can occur at any time and may be made by any party in a transaction. Preparing a bank reconciliation (or "bank rec" for short) is the best way to determine the firm's correct (or actual) cash balance on any particular day.

Some Terminology

Before you start digging through the details, please make sure you understand these terms:

- *Debit memo*—notice from the bank that some amount has been deducted from the firm's account. Examples include:
    - NSF items—checks from customers that have been deposited in the firm's bank account, but were later dishonored ("bounced") by the customer's bank
    - Bank charges/fees—amounts the firm's bank have deducted from the firm's account to pay for some type of bank service
- *Credit memo*—notice from the bank that some amount has been added to the firm's account. Examples include:
    - Interest earned—amounts added to the firm's interest-bearing account
    - Notes collected by the bank—the firm's note receivable from a third party that is collected by the bank on the firm's behalf
- *Outstanding checks*—checks written by the firm that have not cleared the bank as of the bank statement date (result from timing differences)
- *Deposits in transit*—deposits made by the firm that have not cleared the bank as of the bank statement date (result from timing differences)

Reconciliation Procedure

The bank rec has two sections (or "sides"): the book side (the firm's accounting system) and the bank side (balance per the bank). Banks generally prepare monthly statements for its depositors so that all additions to, and deductions from, the accounts can be verified by both entities. With the evolution of the Internet, many depositors interact with the bank (and view their statements) online. This also makes the reconciliation procedure more flexible. Firms no longer have to wait for a monthly statement to prepare a bank rec because their banking transactions are available online at any time.

Bank side:

1. Record the *cash balance per the bank* as of the bank statement date
2. Add: *deposits in transit* (these were already added to the book side and are expected to show up on the bank statement next month)
3. Less: *outstanding checks* (these were already subtracted from the book side and are expected to show up on the bank statement next month)
4. +/–: *bank errors* (these are errors made by the bank. Please read the problem statement carefully to determine if errors made by the bank should be added or subtracted on the bank side)
5. Result—*"actual" cash balance* (also called the adjusted or corrected cash balance) as of the balance sheet date

Book side:

1. Record the *cash balance per books* as of the bank statement date (make sure the dates match!)
2. Add: *bank credit memos* (these were already added to the bank side and will require a journal entry to record them on the book side)
3. Less: *bank debit memos* (these were already subtracted from the bank side and will require a journal entry to record them on the book side)
4. +/–: *book errors* (these are errors made by the firm. Please read the problem statement carefully to determine if errors made on the book side should be added or subtracted on the book side)
5. Result—*"actual" cash balance* (also called the adjusted or corrected cash balance) as of the balance sheet date

NOTE: The amounts calculated in step 5 on both the bank side and the book side should match! If they don't, an error has been made!

If the firm prepares a balance sheet as of the bank statement date, the actual cash balance should be the amount reported as the cash balance on the balance sheet. That means the balance per books must be adjusted to include the reconciling items listed on the book side of the bank rec.

Please keep the following in mind:

- Each journal entry prepared to record a *bank credit memo* requires a DEBIT to cash (to increase the balance per books)
- Each journal entry prepared to record a *bank debit memo* requires a CREDIT to cash (to decrease the balance per books)

Finally, if you are having trouble remembering on which side a reconciling item should be listed on the bank rec, the rule of thumb is that *we list the reconciling item on the side (i.e., bank or book) that has not yet recorded the item.*

PRACTICE 6-1:

Phyllis has called for help again. This time, she's having trouble reconciling Spines' bank count. Can you please help her? Here is the information she's provided. Prepare the bank reconciliation and the appropriate journal entries.

- Balance per bank April 30 $55,000
- Balance per book April 30 $53,965
- Bank service charges $10
- NSF item $3,000
- Deposits in transit $4,000
- Outstanding checks $6,500
- A note receivable for $1,450 plus interest of $75 was collected by the bank. The bank charges $25 for this service
- Error: a check for $3,416 was correctly paid by the bank but was recorded by the company as $3,461. The check was a payment on account.

On a Personal Note

I always encourage my students to pay careful attention to this topic. You can save yourself from paying overdraft fees by actually using the material in this chapter in your day-to-day life. Most of my students have indicated that they have checking accounts (with debit cards an online banking), but fewer than 5% of these students stated that they regularly reconcile their accounts at least monthly. Sometimes, debit card transactions do not clear the bank immediately. Unless you are paying close attention and keeping accurate records, it is very easy to spend cash that is not "really" available. These errors result in very high fees being charged by the bank (possibly $40 per "bounced" transaction. I strongly recommend that you keep a check register (either on paper or electronically) and keep track of when outstanding items clear. This simple process can result in substantial savings.

Demystifying Receivables 7

This chapter covers accounts receivable. Accounts receivable are recorded as the result of transactions with customers. These are referred to as "trade" receivables. A firm may also have notes receivable which may arise from either customer or noncustomer transactions (e.g., loans to employees). Just to clarify, the difference between these two items is that notes receivable are supported by a written, signed, promissory note, while accounts receivable are open accounts.

If you have student loans and/or you've financed an automobile purchase, you are probably familiar with promissory notes. They are documents that summarize the loan details, repayment terms, interest rates, and so forth. If we are the borrower in a transaction, signing such a document results in recording a note payable. If we are the lender, we record a note receivable. Promissory notes may contain wording similar to this:

> *I, [Joe or Mary Student], promise that I will repay the $1 million I am borrowing from ABC Bank to obtain a business degree at XYZ University. I agree to pay a ridiculous amount of interest and that repayment will begin as soon as I walk across the stage at graduation. If I fail to fulfill this obligation, I agree that ABC Bank is allowed to seize all of my personal possessions and that I will voluntarily send my first-born child to gymnastics classes so that s/he can act as the mascot for XYZ University until s/he reaches the age of 25.*

Valuing Accounts Receivable

In this section, we focus on how: (1) various transactions involving accounts receivable are handled in the accounting system; and (2) accounts receivable are presented in the financial statements. We will discuss the following:

1. Writing-off uncollectible accounts
   a. Direct write-off method
   b. Allowance method
2. Estimating bad debt expense (BDE) using an allowance
   a. Percentage of sales method
   b. Percentage of receivables method

Writing-off Uncollectible Accounts

It will probably not surprise you to learn that companies typically do not collect 100 percent of its accounts receivable all of the time. Accounts may become uncollectible for many reasons (e.g., bankruptcy and death). We will discuss two alternative methods.

First, using the direct write-off method means that companies will write-off (i.e., remove the account from the accounting system) uncollectible accounts when the firm determines that the account is uncollectible. The journal entry looks like this:

Bad Debt Expense	$$	
Accounts Receivable		$$

When this entry is posted, it will increase the amount of BDE on the income statement and will decrease the balance of accounts receivable on the balance sheet. The direct write-off method is pretty easy to understand. However, this method has two big flaws. First, the recording of BDE may occur in an accounting period subsequent to the recording of its related revenue (violates the matching principle discussed in chapter 3). Second, since most firms know that they do not historically collect all of their receivables, this method often results in firms overstating their assets by presenting accounts receivable at their gross amount (i.e., 100 percent of the balance). Overstating assets (or income) a BIG no-no in the accounting world! For these reasons, the direct write-off method is not allowed for GAAP.

Instead, we use one of the allowance methods. We set up an account called the allowance for doubtful accounts (ADA). The ADA is classified as a contra-asset account. As a contra-asset, the ADA has a credit balance, the opposite sign of "regular" asset accounts, and its function is to reduce the carrying amount (or book value) of its related asset (accounts receivable in this case). The ADA is presented on the balance sheet as a reduction from gross accounts receivable and the result indicates how much of the receivables the firm actually expects to collect. This number is called the net realizable value or cash realizable value of accounts receivable. Thus, the allowance method allows firms to present accounts receivable at the amount they expect to collect and reduces the likelihood that accounts receivable is overstated.

Using an allowance method requires that firms estimate the amount of uncollectible accounts and BDE for the period. Once determined, the journal entry looks like this:

BDE	$$	
ADA		$$

This entry is posted only at the end of the year. Its purpose is to make sure that BDE is recorded in the same period as its related revenues (fixing the problem with the matching principle). At the same time, the entry increases the balance in the ADA with a credit. Once the ADA is established, it is used to handle cases in which individual accounts become uncollectible. The write-off of uncollectible accounts using an allowance method looks like this:

ADA	$$	
Accounts Receivable		$$

This entry reduces the balances in both the ADA and accounts receivable. Notice that no BDE is recorded when individual accounts are written-off. The BDE was recorded when the revenue was recognized in an earlier accounting period.

If, at some point in the future, an account that had been written-off is subsequently collected (i.e., recovered), the firm must make two journal entries:

First, the firm must reinstate the account by reversing the previous entry:

Accounts Receivable	$$	
ADA		$$

Next, the firm records the cash receipt:

Cash	$$	
Accounts Receivable		$$

This is the same entry we make when normally collecting cash on a customer's account.

Estimating Bad Debt Expense Using an Allowance

We, as human beings, generally lack the gift of being able to see into the future. As a result, corporate management has no way to accurately estimate which customer accounts will become uncollectible in the future. Management will prepare analyses of historical trends to determine their *estimate* of uncollectible accounts. The analyses can be based on one of two financial statement items: (1) credit sales; or (2) accounts receivable.

Using credit sales for analysis means that the firm is using an income statement approach. The focus is on matching revenues with expenses. Management determines an appropriate percentage of sales that is likely to become uncollectible based on past trends. Once determined, that percentage is multiplied by the amount of credit sales. *The dollar amount that results is the amount of BDE to be recorded for the year.* In making this entry, no consideration is given to the balance in the ADA account prior to recording BDE. The ending balance in ADA will be the unadjusted balance plus the amount of BDE recorded for the period.

The other option is to use an analysis of accounts receivable to estimate uncollectible accounts. This is a balance sheet approach, in which the firm is focusing on the net realizable value of accounts receivable. Your homework/test questions might provide you with one percentage of receivables (in total) or they might give you an aging schedule which uses varying percentages based on the age of the balances. Either way, *the dollar amount that results represents the balance the firm needs to have in ADA after the BDE has been posted for the year.* This means we have an extra step to complete: we have to calculate the amount of BDE for the year as the amount required to change the existing balance of the ADA into the desired balance of the ADA.

DEMONSTRATION: Assume that DEF Corp. shows the following financial information as of December 31:

Credit Sales	$100,000
Accounts Receivable	38,000
ADA (unadjusted)	500 credit
Percent sales estimated uncollectible	2%
Percent receivables estimated uncollectible	4%

Record BDE using both the: (A) sales; and (B) receivables methods:

A. $100,000 × .02 = $2,000 (this is the amount of BDE because we used the sales method). Journal entry:

BDE	2,000	
ADA		2,000

Posting:

ADA

Debit	Credit	
	500	Unadj. Bal
	1,020	**JE**
	1,520	Desired Bal

BDE

	Debit	Credit
JE	1,020	

B. $38,000 × .04 = $1,520 (this is the desired balance of the ADA because we used the receivables method). So, we must calculate BDE.

Since the ADA has an unadjusted credit balance, we calculate BDE as the difference between that unadjusted balance and the desired balance: $1,520 – $500 = $1,020:

BDE	1,020	
ADA		1,020

Posting:

But, what happens if the company writes off more uncollectible accounts than it had estimated in the prior year? Well, then the ADA will have a debit balance prior to adjustment. Let's use the same information in the example mentioned earlier, but now assume that the unadjusted ADA balance is a debit of $500:

A. The amount of BDE and the relate journal entry are the same. But, we will see a difference in the ending balance of the ADA:

	Debit	Credit
BDE	2,000	
ADA		2,000

Posting:

ADA

Debit	Credit	
500		Unadj. Bal
	2000	JE
	1,500	**Ending Bal**

BDE

	Debit	Credit
JE	2,000	

B. The desired balance in ADA is the same. However, we need to recalculate the BDE:

	Debit	Credit
BDE	2,020	
ADA		2,020

Posting:

ADA

Debit	Credit	
500		Unadj. Bal
	2,020	**JE**
	1,520	Ending Bal

BDE

	Debit	Credit
JE	2,020	

Notice that the BDE in part B is now higher than it was originally. This is because we are "correcting" the $500 underestimation from the prior year by recording extra BDE in the current year (think about that for a minute).

Inventory Issues 8

So far, we have focused on service companies that earn revenue by providing some type of service to its customers (e.g., advertising). Service companies do not typically carry much (if any) inventory. Now, as we begin to discuss inventory, let's first make sure that we are all using the same definition.

Some Clarification

In this course, the term inventory refers to the items a corporation holds to sell to its customers in order to generate sales revenue. Two types of corporations typically carry inventory: merchandisers and manufacturers. Merchandisers purchase inventory items from other companies and then resell those items to customers. You and I deal with these types of companies on a regular basis. Retailers are merchandisers who sell products directly to the end user (customer). Manufacturers build/make their inventory items and then sell them to customers. In this course, we focus on merchandisers. (Manufacturers are usually covered in a Principles of Accounting II course.)

Calculating Net Income for Merchandising Companies

This section is an introduction to the multistep income statement, which is discussed later in the chapter. When a sale is made, the firm will recognize sales revenue. The next step is to subtract the acquisition cost of the items that were sold from the sales revenue to arrive at gross profit.

Example: ABC Corp. sells five units of inventory at a price of \$7 each. The acquisition cost of those five units was \$3 each.

$$\begin{array}{rl} \text{Sales revenue} = & 5 \times \$7 = \$35 \\ \text{Cost (CGS)} = & 5 \times \$3 = \$15 \\ \hline \text{Gross Profit} = & \$35 - \$15 = \$20 \end{array}$$

We refer to the acquisition cost of the inventory items sold during the accounting period as cost of goods sold (CGS). The CGS account is an expense. Gross profit represents the amount of sales revenue the firm would be able to "keep" before paying any other expenses. In essence, gross profit represents the "mark-up" on the inventory items.

The next step is to subtract the firm's operating expenses from the gross profit. Operating expenses include items such as employee salaries, utilities, repairs and maintenance, and so on. Once all of the expenses have been subtracted from sales revenue, the firm arrives at its net income (or loss) for the period.

Flow of Costs

This portion of the chapter is very important!! VERY important! Please look at the following diagram that presents some key relationships. Understanding these relationships will be a huge help as you work through inventory problems.

Need to Know Box 8-1

FLOW OF COSTS

To begin, please recall that the inventory account is classified as an asset. As we learned earlier, assets are permanent accounts, meaning that they are not closed at the end of the accounting period. Rather, the ending balance from one period becomes the beginning balance for the next period.

Thus, as an accounting period begins, the firm has some amount in its inventory account. We'll call this beginning inventory. As the accounting period continues, the firm will likely acquire more inventory as it is needed. Let's refer to these acquired inventory items as purchases. Hopefully, you will agree with me when I say that adding the cost of the beginning inventory to the cost of purchased items will result in the cost of all of the inventory items the firm had available to sell to its customers during the accounting period. We call this number the cost of goods available for sale. Before going any further, please make sure, this description makes conceptual sense to you and that you are able to follow along with the diagram.

Now, we are going to make an assumption. Unless you are told otherwise, we will assume that no inventory items are stolen, damaged, or otherwise unsellable. Thus, at the end of the accounting period, the goods (inventory) we had available to sell to customers can only be in one of two places: either sold or not sold. If the items were sold, they are in the hands of our customers and their costs are expensed as CGS on the income statement. If they were not sold, the items remain in the firm's possession, and the cost of the items remains on the balance sheet as ending inventory.

If we wanted to show these relationships in the form of mathematical equations, we would have something like this:

$$\text{Beginning Inventory} + \text{Cost of Goods Purchased} = \text{Goods Available for Sale}$$

$$\text{Goods Available for Sale} = \text{Ending Inventory} + \text{Cost of Goods Sold}$$

Therefore, we can also say that the following is true:

$$\text{Beginning Inventory} + \text{Cost of Goods Purchased} = \text{Ending Inventory} + \text{Cost of Goods Sold}$$

Many of the problems you will be solving are based on this relationship. You may be given information for three of these terms and then need to solve for one of them. So, again, please make sure you understand these relationships before you go forward in the chapter.

Inventory Systems

In general, firms choose one of two types of inventory systems: periodic or perpetual. When you consider the word perpetual, you should think of terms like "all of the time," "continuous," and "on-going." Keeping these terms in mind, it should make sense that companies using perpetual inventory systems keep constant track of the balances in their inventory and CGS accounts. When items are sold, the inventory is decreased and CGS is increased. When items are purchased, inventory is increased.

NOTE: Companies that use periodic inventory systems do not keep constant track of the balances in their inventory or CGS accounts. We will focus on the perpetual system.

Purchasing Inventory

Since we are focusing on companies that use perpetual inventory systems, we need to consider which costs to include in the inventory account. The first thing we need to include is the purchase amount per the invoice. The journal entry to record a purchase made on account is:

Inventory	$$	
Accounts Payable		$$

We also need to include a few other costs. One of those is freight costs. This refers to the cost of shipping (e.g., UPS and FedEx). When a buyer pays freight costs, we call it freight-in; and when the seller pays freight costs, we call it freight-out. Freight-in (paid by the buyer) becomes part of the cost of inventory, thus the amount paid for freight-in is debited to the inventory account. When the seller pays freight-out, it is treated as an ordinary expense.

How do companies know who is responsible for paying the freight costs? The answer depends on the freight terms. The two options are (Free on Board) shipping point or FOB destination. These terms indicate when the title (ownership) of the items is transferred from the seller to the buyer. FOB shipping point indicates that the title transfers to the buyer when the seller places them on the "common carrier" (i.e., when the goods are given to the shipping company). Thus, while the items are being transported, they are the property of the buyer, and the buyer pays the freight costs. FOB destination means that the title transfers to the buyer when the items reach the buyer's location (i.e., upon delivery). While the items are in transit, they are the property of the seller and the seller pays the freight.

The next items to be considered are purchase returns and allowances. These arise when an item purchased by the company is sent back to the vendor (return) or when the vendor charges the company a lower price because of a problem (allowance). The effect of recording purchase returns and allowances is to decrease the cost of inventory items. Thus, we debit accounts payable (because the cost of the returned items is no longer due to the seller) and we credit to the inventory account in the journal entry.

Purchase discounts arise when the vendor offers a discount to its customers for prompt payment. For example, assume the payment terms are given as "2/10, n/30." We read this as "two, ten, net 30." These terms indicate that the customer is entitled to a 2 percent discount if payment is received in ten days, with the balance is due in thirty days. When firms take advantage of these money-saving offers, they are, again, decreasing the cost of inventory. Thus, when using a perpetual system, the inventory account is credited when firms are able to take advantage of purchase discounts.

Selling Inventory

Firms using perpetual inventory systems must do two things when sales are made. They must: (1) record the sale and (2) update the balances in the inventory and CGS accounts. If you think about your last trip to Wal-Mart (or wherever you shop), the check-out process likely involved scanning the bar codes of the items you purchased. As the items are scanned, the merchandiser is accomplishing both of these tasks. The amount of sales revenue is recorded (along with your payment method) and the costs of the items you purchased are moved from inventory to CGS.

Recall from the previous section that we discussed purchase returns and allowances along with purchase discounts. Now, we will look at those same transactions from the seller's perspective: sales returns and allowances and sales discounts. Merchandising companies have specific accounts for each of these types of transactions. The "sales returns and allowances" account is debited when the seller receives the returned items (or grants a customer an allowance). The credited account is accounts receivable. This decreases the balance due from the customer. In the case of a sales return, companies using perpetual systems also place the items back into inventory with a debit.

Sales discounts are treated in a similar manner. As customers take advantage of the early-pay discounts, the seller debits the "sales discounts" account. The seller also debits "cash" for the amount received from the customer and credits accounts receivable since the balance is being satisfied.

Multistep Income Statement

Thus far, our discussion of the income statement has focused on the "single-step" format. The calculation of net income is done in one step, that is, total revenues minus

Need to Know Box 8-2

MULTISTEP INCOME STATEMENT

CORPORATION NAME

INCOME STATEMENT

FOR THE PERIOD ENDED DATE

Gross Sales	XX
Sales Discounts	<XX>
Sales Returns and Allowances	<XX>
Net Sales	XX
Cost of Goods Sold	<XX>
Gross Profit	XX
Operating Expenses	<XX>
Income <Loss> from Operations	XX
Other Revenues and Gains	XX
Other Expenses and Losses	<XX>
Income before Taxes	XX
Income Tax Expense	<XX>
Net Income <Loss>	XX

total expenses. While this gives the financial statement reader the results of operations for the period, the single-step income statement lacks certain financial information that might also be useful in assisting potential creditors and/or investors with their resource allocation decisions.

The multistep income statement is just that. Net income is calculated as a result of multiple "steps" (or intermediate calculations). The amount of net income or loss is the same for both the single- and multistep formats. This is because, in both cases, we are subtracting total expenses from total revenues. However, in the multistep version, we are "grouping" the contents of the income statement into different categories.

The first thing we do on a multistep income statement is calculate net sales. We arrive at this figure by subtracting sales discounts and sales returns and allowances from gross sales revenue. From net sales, we subtract CGS to arrive at gross profit (as discussed earlier).

The next section lists the operating expenses for the period. These represent the cost incurred by the firm for the purpose of generating revenue during the accounting period. After subtracting total operating expenses from net sales, we get income (or loss) from operations (also called operating income [or loss]). As the name implies, this figure represents only the financial results of the firm's operating activities during the period. It does not include amounts that may arise from the firm's other activities (e.g., sales of assets, interest earned on investments).

Next, we have the nonoperating section of the income statement. Here is where we see the results of activities that do not pertain directly to the firm's main business function. The two subheadings typically shown are "Other Revenues and Gains" (which are added to operating income) and "Other Expenses and Losses" (which are subtracted from operating income). The result is "Income before Taxes." Next, we calculate income tax, and finally, we reach the bottom line: net income or net loss.

Determining Ownership of Goods

Earlier, we discussed "goods in transit" along with the terms FOB shipping point and FOB destination. I'll ask you to refer to your textbook and notes if you have remaining questions on this.

The next topic in this section is "consignment." In a consignment agreement, one company (Company A) places its inventory with another company (Company B). Company B agrees to sell the inventory on behalf of Company A, and will keep a percentage of the selling price as commission. Key items of note regarding these arrangements:

- Company B does not purchase the inventory from Company A
- Company A maintains ownership of the inventory items, even though Company B has physical custody of the inventory items.

Thus, on the balance sheet date, the consigned goods will be shown as current assets on Company A's balance sheet. Company B will not include the consigned goods on its balance sheet. Watch for specific terminology. For a given firm:

- Goods "out on" consignment belong to the firm and should be included on as inventory on its balance sheet.
- Goods "held on" consignment belong to someone else and should not be included as inventory on its balance sheet.

Inventory Costing

In many industries, it is not possible to specifically identify which inventory items are sold at a particular time. This is because many merchandisers (e.g., Office Depot, Wal-Mart) purchase large volumes of identical inventory items at various costs during an accounting period.

For example, consider a firm that had a total of 1,000 units available to sell during the accounting period. At the end of the year, 450 units remain unsold (as ending inventory) and 550 units have been sold. (Please refer to the relationships demonstrated in earlier if this description is not clear). Also assume that the units available for sale during the year were acquired for four different unit costs.

When this firm sells the inventory, it must have a way to determine the costs associated with ending inventory and CGS. In order to do this, the firm makes an "assumption" about how costs flow through the accounting system. This assumption is for accounting purposes only and does not have to match the actual physical flow of inventory.

We cover three cost flow assumptions:

- *First in, first out (FIFO)*: We presume the items are sold in the order in which they were purchased. Think of FIFO as a water pipe: the water flows into one end of the pipe and out the other. The first drops that go into the pipe will be the first ones out of the pipe.
- *Last in, first out (LIFO)*: We presume the items are sold in the opposite order in which they were purchased. Think of LIFO as a hay stack. As a farmer gets more hay, he piles it on top of the hay he already had. As he uses the hay, he takes it off of the top of the stack.
- *Average Cost*: We calculate an average unit cost (total cost divided by total units available) and that average cost is used to calculate the cost of ending inventory and CGS.

As with the other topics we've covered so far, mastery of these concepts requires repeated practice. Your text likely provides several examples on this topic and I recommend that you work through them on your own to make sure you understand where the numbers are coming from.

Also, you should always make sure, you know the following information before you start performing a bunch of calculations: (1) the cost flow assumption to be used and (2) what the problem is asking you to calculate. Some problems ask for the cost of ending inventory, some ask for CGS, and some may even ask for gross profit (sales minus CGS). Be clear about these items before punching your calculator keys so that you don't accidently calculate the wrong figure.

Lower of Cost or Market

This last topic is (I think) pretty straightforward. When preparing the balance sheet, we must be very careful about the valuation of our assets. Accountants take a conservative approach. Specifically, we strive for correctness; but if an error is made, we'd prefer for that error not to overstate (inflate) the firm's assets or net income.

Keeping this in mind, we must check our inventory for obsolescence and/or permanent loss of value at the end of each accounting period. We compare the inventory's cost to its market value, and we present the inventory using the value that is lower. For each inventory item, cost is compared to market and the lowest value is selected for balance sheet presentation. Yes, it's just that simple.

What Depreciation Is (and Is Not) 9

I'll begin this discussion by giving a brief overview of what depreciation is and how it is accounted for. Then we will dig into some details to determine how depreciation is calculated.

Depreciation

In Chapter 3, we discussed adjusting entries: accruals and deferrals. If you look back at that chapter, you will see that the topic of depreciation was included in the "deferred (prepaid) expenses" section. We said that these adjustments are made when the firm pays for a something up-front and then uses it over some period of time. The depreciation entry is a special case of a prepaid (deferred) expense adjustment. As a long-term operating asset (e.g., vehicle and building) is used, we record depreciation expense that reflects the cost incurred by the firm while using the asset to generate revenue.

One of the issues that students sometimes have in this course is that they often begin their accounting class with an "economic" definition of depreciation in mind. For many people, the word depreciation implies a loss or reduction in value. In accounting, however, this is not the case. For this course, the term depreciation refers to the systematic allocation of the cost of a long-term asset to the periods of time in which it is used to generate revenue. Recording depreciation expense helps us follow the matching principle, that is, recording expense in the same period with its related revenue.

The journal entry for recording depreciation looks like this (always the same format):

Depreciation Expense	$$	
Accumulated Depreciation		$$

The depreciation expense account is an operating expense and will appear on the income statement. The accumulated depreciation account is classified as a contra-asset on the balance sheet. Its function is to lower the book value of its related asset to reflect the amount of the acquisition cost that has not yet been "used up." Book value is calculated as follows:

Acquisition Cost – Accumulated Depreciation = Book Value

GAAP allows firms to use one of several different methods to calculate their depreciation expense. We will discuss three:

1. Straight-line
2. Units of activity
3. Double declining balance

Required Information

In order to calculate depreciation, we need three pieces of information:

- (Acquisition) cost—how much was paid to obtain the asset
- Useful life—an estimate of the asset's total productivity. It may be given in turns of time (some number of years) or in terms of output (some number of units)
- Salvage (or residual) value—an estimate of what the value of the asset will be at the end of its useful life
    - NOTE: subtracting salvage value from cost results in the depreciable cost or depreciable base. This figure represents the total amount of depreciation the firm plans to record over the asset's useful life.

Straight-Line Depreciation

The straight-line method is the easiest option for calculating depreciation expense. The underlying presumption is that the asset will be used at a steady rate over its useful life. The calculation is:

$$\frac{(\text{Cost} - \text{Salvage Value})}{\text{Useful Life (years)}} = \text{Annual Depreciation Expense}$$

This method allocates depreciation as an equal amount each year of the asset's useful life. We call it "straight line" because a graph of depreciation expense over time results in a straight line (amazing right?).

Note that the calculation results in annual depreciation expense. This refers to a twelve-month year. If the firm did not have or use the asset for the full year, the annual depreciation expense calculation has to be adjusted to reflect the time period in which the asset was actually in use. For example, for a calendar-year firm, an asset acquired on May 1, should only be depreciated from May 1 to December 31. Hence, the firm would multiply the annual depreciation expense by the fraction (8/12) because the asset was only in use for eight months of the year.

Units of Activity Depreciation

This method is similar to straight line in the sense that we calculate depreciation based on the expected usefulness of the asset. However, with units of activity, we must first calculate the depreciation rate as a function of total units of expected output. Once we have the rate, we use it to calculate the total depreciation expense using the asset's actual output for the accounting period. The calculations look like this:

#1 – calculate depreciation rate:

$$\frac{\text{(Cost – Salvage Value)}}{\text{Useful Life (units)}} = \text{(\$ / unit) Depreciation Rate}$$

#2 – calculate depreciation expense:

$$\text{Actual Output} \times \text{Depreciation Rate} = \text{Depreciation Expense}$$

Because the actual output for an asset normally varies from year to year, the units of activity method produces a variable amount of depreciation expense over time.

Double Declining Balance Depreciation

The rationale for this type of depreciation is that assets tend to be more productive when they are new and less productive as they age (think about your car). Declining balance depreciation is what we call an accelerated method because we record more depreciation expense in the earlier years of use an then progressively less as the asset ages.

One big difference between this method (double declining balance [DDB]) and the ones we discussed earlier is that DDB begins with the asset's book value (described earlier). We then multiply the book value times double the straight-line depreciation rate. Here is the calculation:

$$\text{Book Value} \times \frac{2}{\text{Useful Life (years)}} = \text{Annual Depreciation Expense}$$

The depreciation rate (2 divided by the useful life) is where the straight-line rate is doubled. Recall the earlier mentioned straight-line formula. We can restate this equation as:

$$\frac{\text{(Cost-Salvage Value)}}{\text{Useful Life (years)}} = \text{(Cost-Salvage Value)} \times \frac{1}{\text{Useful Life (years)}}$$

Thus, dividing 2 by the useful life under the DDB method results in doubling the straight-line rate. Try this out using five years as the useful life.

Notice that the salvage value is not included in this computation. However, before recording the annual depreciation expense as calculated, we must make sure that the resulting (new) book value does not drop below the salvage value.

Liabilities (We Owe, We Owe, So Off We Go ...) 10

Overview

The first section of Chapter 10 is really a collection of many topics. What each of the topics has in common is that they are recorded as current (short-term) liabilities on the balance sheet. These amounts that the firm owes (i.e., debts) that are due within one year.

Notes Payable

Notes payable may be short- or long-term in nature. In this chapter, we focus on the short-term notes. We discussed notes payable briefly in Chapter 8. Now we will focus on one aspect of notes payable: interest expense.

Interest is the cost of borrowing. We can incur interest expense (as the borrower) or we can earn interest revenue (as the lender). Either way, the calculation is the same:

$$\text{Principal} \times \text{Interest Rate} \times \text{Time} = \text{Interest}$$

For purposes of your homework and test questions, you should assume that the interest rates you are given are annual rates (12 months) unless you're told otherwise. Most students do well with identifying the principal and the interest rate in the word problems. The trouble spot seems to be the time element. Interest expense (or revenue) is *always calculated based on the amount of time the principal was outstanding in the accounting period.*

Example: JKL Corp. signed a $100,000, five-month, 8 percent note payable on October 1, 2015. Calculate the interest expense to be accrued at December 31, 2014.

- Principal = $100,000
- Interest Rate = 8 percent (per year)
- Time = three months
  - The note was signed on October 1 and the accounting period ends on December 31. Thus, the note was outstanding for three months in 2014. The remaining two months of interest expense (January and February) will be recorded in 2015.

$$\text{Calculation}: \$100,000 \times .08 \times (3/12) = \$2,000$$

December 31, 2014 Journal Entry:

Interest Expense	2,000	
Interest Payable		2,000

Sales Tax

All of us have paid sales tax. When we shop, we check out at the register and sales tax is automatically added to the total of our purchases. So, why is the topic included in this chapter? Because as we pay sales tax on our purchases, the retailer collects the funds and is required to remit them to the state taxing authority. Thus, the sales tax collected does not belong to retailer. Rather, the retailer must keep track of sales taxes collected separately from its sales revenue. The retailer record these amounts as sales tax payable, which is classified as a current liability.

You will encounter two types of sales tax problems. In the first type, sales and sales taxes are segregated (separated) by the retailer. Typically, the problem states the amount of revenue and the sales tax rate to be applied. This problem requires a quick calculation to arrive at the amount of sales tax:

$$\text{Sales Revenue} \times \text{Sales Tax Rate} = \text{Sales Tax}$$

In the other type of problem, the retailer does not segregate sales revenue and sales tax. In these problems, you are given the total amount collected by the retailer and that the amount includes sales tax. When solving, you must first determine how much of the collections represent revenue and how much is sales tax. Your calculation will look like this:

$$\frac{\text{Total Collections}}{1+\text{Sales Tax Rate}} = \text{Sales Revenue}$$

Once you've calculated the amount of sales revenue, you should be able to determine the amount of sales tax included with the collections.

Regardless of the type of problem, the journal entry will look like this:

Cash (collections)	$$	
Sales Tax Payable		$$
Sales Revenue		$$

Payroll and Payroll Taxes

I'm sure that you have wondered (at least once) why your paycheck is not as large as you'd expected. If you look at the stub, you'll see items described as "withholding." These are amounts that your employer deducts from your gross pay to arrive at your net pay (the amount of your check). While the employer holds on to these amounts, they must be recorded as liabilities because they must be turned over to the appropriate company or taxing authority, depending on why the withheld item was withheld.

Payroll deductions can be classified as mandatory or voluntary. Mandatory deductions are required by law. The mandatory deductions are:

- Federal income tax
- State income tax
- City/local income tax (as applicable)
- Social Security and Medicare (Federal Insurance Contributions Act - FICA) tax

Voluntary deductions are the amounts we *ask* our employer to withhold for us. These deductions may include items such as:

- Charitable contributions
- Union dues
- Insurance premiums
- Retirement savings

When recording payroll in the accounting system, the amount debited to salary and wage expense is the gross amount of earnings. From that figure, all of the items being withheld are subtracted and credited to the appropriate liability accounts. They will be paid to the appropriate parties at a future date. The final credit in the entry will either be to cash (if the employees are being paid at that time) or salary and wages payable (if employees will be paid on another day).

Employers are also required to pay payroll taxes. The law requires that employers pay FICA taxes in the same amount as was withheld from the employees. The firm is also required to pay federal and state unemployment taxes. The employer does not pay income taxes for its employees.

Unearned Revenue

This topic was discussed in Chapter 3, when we focused on deferred revenues. Please review Chapter 3, in addition to the appropriate sections of your text, if you need to review this item.

Current Maturities of Long-Term Debt

This item is purely a classification issue. No journal entries are needed. The concept is that the portion of long-term debt that will be due within the next year should be classified as current liabilities on the balance sheet. The remaining portion of the debt should remain in the long-term liabilities section. That's pretty much it.

SECTION TWO

A FEW MORE THINGS

Practice Solutions 11

PRACTICE 1-1 SOLUTION

SPINES, INC.
TRANSACTION ANALYSIS

DATE	ASSETS	=	LIABILITIES	+	S/H EQUITY
01-Jan	+$50,000				+$50,000
	Cash				Common Stock
02-Jan	Not a transaction.				
03-Jan	<$2,400>				
	Cash				
	+$2,400				
	Prepaid Insurance				
07-Jan	+$10,000		+10,000		
	Furniture		Accounts Payable		
	+25,000				
	Equipment				
	<$25,000>				
	Cash				
10-Jan	+5,000		+$5,000		
	Supplies		Accounts Payable		
25-Jan	<$10,000>		<$10,000>		
	Cash		Accounts Payable		

(*Continued*)

(*Continued*)

SPINES, INC.
TRANSACTION ANALYSIS

DATE	ASSETS	=	LIABILITIES	+	S/H EQUITY
30-Jan	+$30,000 Cash +$8,000 Accounts Receivable				+$38,000 Service Revenue
	<$8,000> Cash				<$8,000> Salary and Wage Expense
	<$2,000> Cash				<$2,000> Dividends

PRACTICE 2-1 SOLUTION

SPINES, INC.
GENERAL JOURNAL

Date	Accounts	Debit	Credit
1-Jan	Cash	50,000	
	Common Stock		50,000
02-Jan	No entry needed for hiring employees		
03-Jan	Prepaid Insurance	2,400	
	Cash		2,400
07-Jan	Furniture	10,000	
	Accounts Payable		10,000
	Equipment	25,000	
	Cash		25,000

10-Jan	Supplies	5,000	
	Accounts Payable		5,000
25-Jan	Accounts Payable	10,000	
	Cash		10,000
30-Jan	Cash	30,000	
	Accounts Receivable	8,000	
	Service Revenue		38,000
30-Jan	Salary and Wages Expense	8,000	
	Cash		8,000
30-Jan	Dividends	2,000	
	Cash		2,000

SPINES, INC.
GENERAL LEDGER

CASH		FURNITURE		DIVIDENDS	
50,000	2,400	10,000		2,000	
30,000	25,000				
	10,000				
	8,000				
	2,000				
32,600					

(Continued)

(*Continued*)

SPINES, INC.
GENERAL LEDGER

ACC RECEIVABLE	
8,000	

EQUIPMENT	
25,000	

SERVICE REVENUE	
	38,000

SUPPLIES	
5,000	

ACC PAYABLE	
10,000	10,000
	5,000
	5,000

SAL and WAGE EXP	
8,000	

PREPAID INS	
2,400	

COMMON STOCK	
	50,000

PRACTICE 2-2 SOLUTION

SPINES, INC.
UNADJUSTED TRIAL BALANCE
FOR THE MONTH ENDED JANUARY 31

Cash	32,600	
Accounts Receivable	8,000	
Supplies	5,000	
Prepaid Insurance	2,400	
Furniture	10,000	
Equipment	25,000	
Accounts Payable		5,000
Common Stock		50,000
Dividends	2,000	
Service Revenue		38,000
Salary and Wage Expense	8,000	
	93,000	93,000

PRACTICE 3-1 SOLUTION

This error has two effects:

1. Revenue of $1,500 of service revenue is reported twice; and,
2. The balance in the customer's account receivable does not get updated. During the next billing cycle, the customer would receive another invoice for $1,500 which had already been paid.

PRACTICE 3-2 SOLUTION

This error has two effects:

1. Utility expense of $350 is reported twice; and,
2. The balance in the painter's account payable does not get updated. During the next payment cycle, the painter might accidently pay the utility bill twice.

PRACTICE 3-3 SOLUTION

SPINES, INC.
GENERAL JOURNAL

Date	Accounts	Debit	Credit
31-Jan	Depreciation Expense	50	
	Accumulated Depreciation-Furn		50
31-Jan	Depreciation Expense	100	
	Accumulated Depreciation-Equip		100
31-Jan	Supplies Expense	1,500	
	Supplies		1,500
31-Jan	Telephone Expense	80	
	Utilities Expense	250	
	Accounts Payable		330
31-Jan	Insurance Expense	200	
	Prepaid Insurance		200

Notes:

- One month of depreciation expense is calculated by dividing the annual depreciation by twelve months
- The amount of supplies expense represents the amount of supplies used during the month of January
- The insurance expense is calculated by dividing the full premium of $2,400 by the twelve-month coverage term.

SPINES, INC.
GENERAL LEDGER

CASH		FURNITURE		SUPPLIES EXPENSE	
50,000	2,400	10,000		1,500	
30,000	25,000				
	10,000				
	8,000				
	2,000				
32,600					

ACC RECEIVABLE	
8,000	

EQUIPMENT	
25,000	

SAL and WAGE EXP	
8,000	

SUPPLIES	
5,000	1,500
	3,500

ACC PAYABLE	
10,000	10,000
	5,000
	330
	5,330

DEPRECIATION EXP	
50	
100	

PREPAID INS	
2,400	200

COMMON STOCK	
	50,000

TELEPHONE EXP	
80	

(Continued)

(*Continued*)

SPINES, INC.
GENERAL LEDGER

ACCUM. DEPR.-FURN	
	50

DIVIDENDS	
2,000	

UTILITY EXPENSE	
250	

ACCM. DEPR.-EQUIP	
	100

SERVICE REVENUE	
	38,000

INSURANCE EXPENSE	
200	

ACCUM. DEPR.-FUR = accumulated depreciation-furniture; ACCM. DEPR.-EQUIP = accumulated depreciation-equipment; EXP = expense.

SPINES, INC.
ADJUSTED TRIAL BALANCE
FOR THE MONTH ENDED JANUARY 31

Account	Debit	Credit
Cash	32,600	
Accounts Receivable	8,000	
Supplies	3,500	
Prepaid Insurance	2,200	
Furniture	10,000	
Accum. Depr.-Furn		50
Equipment	25,000	
Accum. Depr.-Equip		100
Accounts Payable		5,330
Common Stock		50,000
Dividends	2,000	
Service Revenue		38,000
Depreciation Expense	150	
Supplies Expense	1,500	
Insurance Expense	200	
Telephone Expense	80	
Utility Expense	250	
Salary and Wage Expense	8,000	
	93,480	93,480

PRACTICE 4-1 SOLUTION

SPINES, INC.
INCOME STATEMENT
FOR THE MONTH ENDED JANUARY 31

Service Revenue		$ 38,000
Expenses:		
Depreciation Expense	$ 150	
Supplies Expense	1,500	
Insurance Expense	200	
Telephone Expense	80	
Utility Expense	250	
Salary and Wage Expense	8,000	(10,180)
Net Income		**$ 27,820**

SPINES, INC.
STATEMENT OF RETAINED EARNINGS
FOR THE MONTH ENDED JANUARY 31

Beginning Balance	$ -
Net Income	27,820
Dividends	(2,000)
Ending Balance	**$ 25,820**

SPINES, INC.
BALANCE SHEET
AS OF JANUARY 31

Assets:		
Cash		$ 32,600
Accounts Receivable		8,000
Supplies		3,500
Prepaid Insurance		2,200
Furniture	$ 10,000	
Accum. Depr.-Furn	(50)	9,950
Equipment	25,000	
Accum. Depr.-—Equip	(100)	24,900
Total Assets		**$ 81,150**
Liabilities and Stockholders' Equity		
Accounts Payable		$ 5,330
Common Stock		50,000
Retained Earnings		25,820
Total Liabilities and Stockholders' Equity		**$ 81,150**

PRACTICE 5-1 SOLUTION

SPINES, INC.
GENERAL JOURNAL

Date	Accounts	Debit	Credit
31-Jan	Service Revenue	38,000	
	Income Summary		38,000
31-Jan	Income Summary	10,180	
	Depreciation Expense		150
	Supplies Expense		1,500
	Insurance Expense		200
	Telephone Expense		80
	Utility Expense		250
	Salary and Wage Expense		8,000
31-Jan	Income Summary	27,820	
	Retained Earnings		27,820
31-Jan	Retained Earnings	2,000	
	Dividends		2,000

SPINES, INC.
POST-CLOSING TRIAL BALANCE
AS OF JANUARY 31

Account	Debit	Credit
Cash	32,600	
Accounts Receivable	8,000	
Supplies	3,500	
Prepaid Insurance	2,200	
Furniture	10,000	
Accum. Depr.—Furn		50
Equipment	25,000	
Accum. Depr.—Equip		100
Accounts Payable		5,330
Common Stock		50,000
Retained Earnings		25,820
	81,300	81,300

PRACTICE 6-1 SOLUTION

BANK RECONCILIATION

APRIL 30

PER BANK		**PER BOOKS**	
Balance, April 30	55,000	Balance, April 30	53,965
Add: Deposits in Transit	4,000	Add: Check Error	45
		Note Collected by Bank	1,525
Less: Outstanding Checks	(6,500)	Less: NSF Check	(3,000)
		Bank Service Charges	(35)
Adjusted Balance	**52,500**	Adjusted Balance	**52,500**

SPINES, INC.
GENERAL JOURNAL

Date	Accounts	Debit	Credit
30-Apr	Cash	45	
	Accounts Payable		45
30-Apr	Cash	1,525	
	Interest Revenue		75
	Note Receivable		1,450
30-Apr	Accounts Receivable	3,000	
	Cash		3,000
30-Apr	Bank Charges	35	
	Cash		35

Suggested Study Plan 12

The keys to doing well in accounting classes are:

- Attending class regularly
- Proper preparation for class
- Keeping current with course material
- Asking good questions and using your new accounting vocabulary
- Repeated practice of accounting problems

You are strongly encouraged to *resist the temptation to memorize step-by-step procedures* when solving accounting problems. Instead, you should *strive to understand the principles and concepts* underlying the accounting problems. By doing so, you will be able to analyze each problem to arrive at the proper solution without memorizing steps.

This study plan is intended to help you properly prepare for accounting classes. These steps are merely *suggestions*. You are encouraged to use this plan as a starting point and then modify/adapt the plan to suit your individual learning style. *You should expect to spend a minimum of ten hours per week outside of class to earn a C or better in this course.*

Note that many of the steps outlined in this study plan can be applied to other courses.

Preparing for Lecture (to be completed *BEFORE* class)

- Review the "Study Objectives" and "Preview" at the beginning of each chapter (ten minutes):
    - Get an idea of what will be covered and how the chapter is organized
    - Being aware of the main topics that will be covered in the chapter will help you to focus your reading
- Read the chapter *in detail*, one section at a time (2–3 hours)
    - Pay attention to terms in bold-face
    - Highlight/under line important concepts

      Note: Please don't rely on highlights made by other people. If you purchased a used book that is already highlighted, you should highlight/underline the items you feel are most important in a different color.
    - Make notes in the margins to clarify material or indicate items that are confusing
    - Takes notes—summarize concepts in your own words
    - Rework any problems that are presented in the chapter to test your understanding

- Work through each example within the chapter (1/2–1 hour)
  - These examples give you practice in applying the concepts discussed in the chapter up to that point.
  - Try to solve them without looking at the solutions. If you get stuck, look at the solution and then reread that section of the chapter to *understand why* your answer was incorrect.
  - Make sure you understand the material in that section *before you go on!!!!*
- *Attend class*:
  - Ask the questions you were unable to clarify on your own
  - Take good notes

Postlecture Review (to be completed *as soon as possible* after class)

- Look over your reading notes and your lecture notes; consolidate your two sets of notes into one (1–2 hours)
- Review the study objectives and/or glossary at the end of the chapter; reread chapter sections that are still confusing (1–2 hours)
- Work through any comprehensive problems at the end of the chapter (1/2 hour)

Preparing for Homework Problem Review (to be completed *BEFORE* class)

- Work each problem *without looking at the solution* (2–3 hours)
- Look at the solution to determine where errors occurred. For problems you did not do correctly, go back and *figure out WHY your answer was wrong* (1–2 hours)
  - Figuring out "why" is where most of the learning takes place!!
  - Make note of any issues you were unable to resolve on your own
- *Attend class*:
  - Ask the questions you were unable to clarify on your own
  - Take good notes

Post-homework Problem Review (to be completed *as soon as possible* after class)

- Look over your notes from class and rework the problems without looking at the solutions. Note any remaining problems and bring them up during the next class or in office hours (one to two hours)
- Do any self-study questions at the end of the chapter without looking at the solutions (1/2–1 hour)
  - Review the appropriate chapter section for each question you get wrong,
  - Take notes.

- Read through the "questions" at the end of the chapter without looking at the solutions (1/2–1 hour)
    - These questions test your understanding of the concepts and principles discussed in the chapter
    - Determine how prepared you would be to answer the questions. For those that give you pause, go back and review the appropriate sections before moving on to the next chapter.

Preparing for Exams

- Begin this process at least one week before the exam. You will then have enough time to ask your instructor for any additional help you may need. *Do not wait until the day before the exam to seek assistance.*
- If you have followed this study plan, you should only need to review the material and not "cram" for the exam:
    - Review notes and slides; make sure you understand the concepts
    - Reread the questions at the end of each chapter. This will help you determine your level of understanding. If you can't answer something, be sure to reread the appropriate sections of the chapter.
- Rework the assigned problems:
    - Do not rely on the solutions manual while working problems
    - Resist the urge to memorize steps in solving problems
- Practice additional problems:
    - Locate relevant problems in your text that were not assigned
    - Check your work with the solutions manual. Identify errors and why they occurred.
    - Work the problems again as necessary

www.ingramcontent.com/pod-product-compliance
Lightning Source LLC
La Vergne TN
LVHW082356200926
848481LV00012B/3582

* 9 7 8 1 5 2 4 9 1 6 5 1 0 *